Flatford

Constable Country

Ian St.John

Painting is but another word for feeling. I associate my 'careless boyhood' with all that lies on the banks of the Stour. They made me a painter, and I am grateful, that is, I had often thought of pictures of them before I had ever touched a pencil
John Constable in his letter to John Fisher 23 Oct. 1821

Suffolk Walker

Flatford Map

Contents

The Flatford Map on the opposite page has numbers on it locating the views painted by John Constable in his famous pictures. Each number refers to a page in this book where you will find the painting. To look at the full-page landscape paintings, turn the book sideways and hold the upper page a little off vertical, as if it were on an easel, then read the text on the page below. There are also numbers on the map referring to pages discussing interesting features of the hamlet.

R B Beckett commented about John Constable
"His earliest memories were a blend of wide and distant views over the valley which has for its centre the noble tower of Dedham Church, of the moving clouds above, of upland woods and fields running down in gentle declivities, and of a winding stream where small boys would fish in summer from the locks, under the shade of overhanging trees. Of all these memories, the one which seems to have left the deepest impression on his mind was the busy scene round Flatford Mill, with the constant procession of barges stopping to load or unload their cargo". John Constable's Correspondence: The Family at East Bergholt 1801-1837 page 10

The Haywain

John Constable 1821 Oil Painting 130.5 x 185.5cm (51¼ x 73in) National Gallery London

It is noon on a summer's day. A driver and boy are taking the empty haywain across the flat ford to collect hay from the distant meadow. The boy is calling to a spaniel that is padding along the gravel bank, known locally at that time as 'the shingle'. River Stour was tidal to the lower gates of Flatford Lock and below Flatford Mill. Wheelmarks made by the haywain along the shingle will be washed away by the next high tide. The oil sketch (fig. 1) of Willy Lott's House shows the shingle covered by a high tide.

The haywain has ventured upon the mill-stream ford and turned sharp left. With front wheels turned to the right, its three black horses with their distinctive red-felt wither pads are about to veer right and pull the wain through the water-filled gap. Crossing the river Stour ford, the team will pull it out of the water on to Mill Meadow. Making its way across the meadow, man and boy will greet the reapers in Abram Constable's Foxes Meadow before continuing to John Lott's meadow, named, with good humour, Uplands. The wain will be loaded with sun-dried hay and make the return journey over meadows and ford to John Lott's barns in the yard at Valley Farm. William Brasier's map (page 13) shows Valley Farm on both sides of the Stour.

Next to Willy Lott's House, to the right of the flowering elderberry bush and the brick bread oven, a kitchen maid kneels on the landing stage. Unconcerned by the haywain, and with one clay pitcher by her side, she steadies herself by the handrail and scoops a pitcher of fresh water from the mill-stream.

Having left the security afforded by the Millhouse forecourt wall, a keen angler is pushing through the undergrowth to the rowing boat moored by the water's edge. Constable copied his drawing of the rowing boat (fig. 2) made ten years earlier. Flatford Mill is grinding corn using power generated by the right-hand of two water-wheels situated inside the mill (page 11). This water-wheel sends turbulent white water (seen in the foreground of the painting) out of the culvert into the mill-stream. The angler can hear the regular plashing of the water-wheel. Once aboard the boat he will row downstream to fish in peace.

1 *Willy Lott's House* John Constable 1811
Oil sketch 27.3 x 24.2cm (10¾ x 9½in)
V&A Picture Library London

2 *A rowing boat moored by a river bank*
John Constable 1809 Black Chalk Sketch
9 x 12.6cm (3½ x 5in) Witt Collection
Courtauld Institute Galleries London

3 Willy Lott's House Pre-late 1920's photograph Colchester Museum

4 Willy Lott's House cut-away Robert Cook

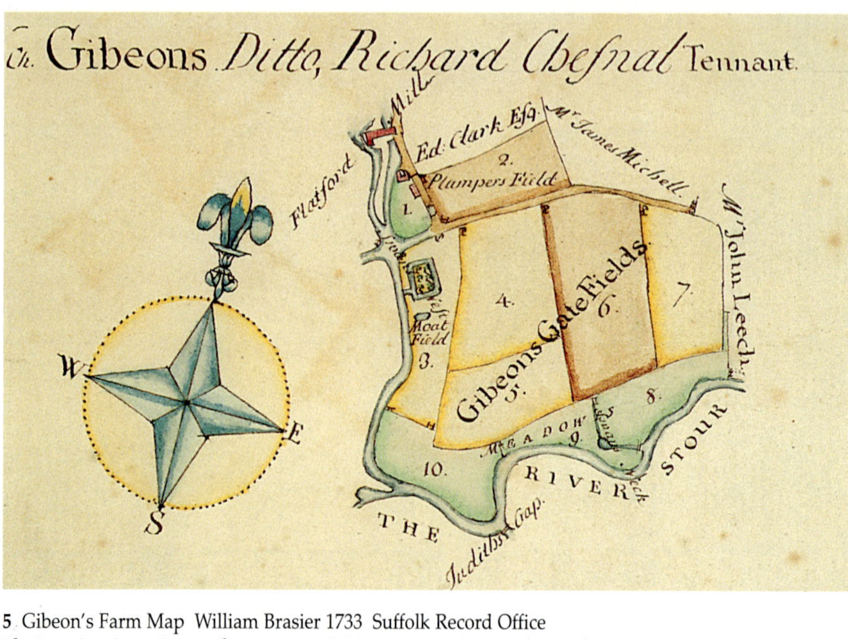

5 Gibeon's Farm Map William Brasier 1733 Suffolk Record Office
The Lott family took over the tenancy of Gibeons Farm from Richard Chesnal.

Willy Lott's House

William Lott (1761 - 1849) was a farmer who worked the 39 acre Gibeon's Farm (fig. 5 & Flatford Map page 2 - the lake was added later). At first he was a tenant farmer. Then, in 1825, he bought the farm. He lived in the farmhouse which has come to be called 'Willy Lott's House'. William Lott remained a bachelor and may have had difficulties learning because his elder brother, John, did his accounts and John Constable's sister Mary, living in Flatford Millhouse, wrote a letter to her brother dated 1 March 1825 saying Mr. Lott *"sometimes shed tears in his old age that he was left untaught by those who had charge of him in his youth"*. Willy Lott rarely left the parish and was buried in the local churchyard.

What appears to be a small single-storey timber-framed extension on the right front of the building is in fact a **late-medieval building** which stood on its own, long before the rest of Willy Lott's House was built. Figure 4 shows it to be a substantial, closely studded building raised on a brick plinth. The gable-end window has two wooden diamond-sectioned mullions.

The **two-storey wing** on the left was built as a separate building in the seventeenth century. The red brick inglenook fireplace and chimney stack in figure 4 was originally outside the building against the wall. It was then removed and rebuilt in its present position.

Later in the seventeenth century, the **back range** was built joining the two buildings. It is mid-way in height, consisting of one storey with attic rooms.

A brick **bread oven** was attached to the right gable-end against the chimney stack which drew away smoke. The oven is seen in *The Haywain* (opposite page 5) and in the old photograph (fig. 3).

Haywain

The 1808 drawing of a timber wagon by William Henry Pyne (fig. 6) is similar to Constable's haywain painted in 1821 (fig. 7).

The haywain was a converted timber wagon. Both wagons have heavy rectangular stocks above the axles that helped distribute the weight of the load of timber. Both also have a central undercarriage beam along which the rear axle and wheels were moved, to accommodate different lengths of timber.

To contain hay, the 'haywain' was loosely boarded across the top of the stocks and sides were attached.

6 Timber Wagon William Henry Pyne 1808 Luton Museum

7 DETAIL *The Haywain* John Constable 1821 National Gallery London

Flatford

The haywain is crossing the ford below Flatford Mill.

The hamlet of Flatford derives its name from this hard level ford (fig. 8). During winter storms, huge volumes of water rush down the river, carrying a gravel-sand load that scours the mill-stream pool and lock millpool. Rushed along by the strong river current, the load is deposited forcefully (hydraulic compaction) in the mill-stream and into the river below Flatford Lock as a broad shoal, giving a compact and level surface of gravel - the flat ford.

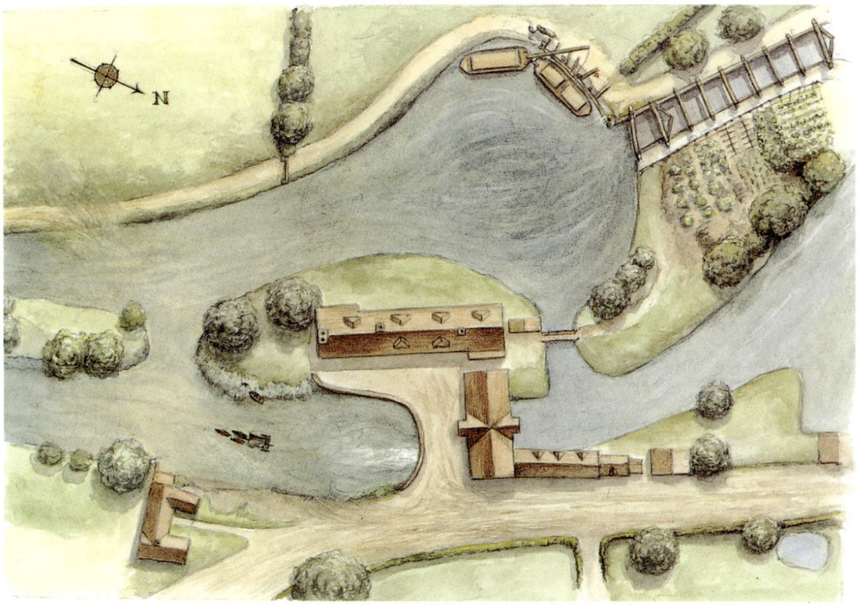

8 Bird's-eye view of the flat ford during Constable's time Robert Cook

9 Willy Lott's House today

Flatford Mill from Willy Lott's House

John Constable 1811 Oil Painting 16.5 x 30cm (6½ x 11¾in) Paul Mellon Collection Virginia

This is the only known painting by John Constable of Flatford Mill from this viewpoint. On the left edge of the painting, Willy Lott's House has an open first-floor window. Flatford Millhouse is the prominent warm brick building left of centre. Except for the removal of two dormer windows, it has changed little since Georgian times. Flatford Mill to the right of the Millhouse is partly obscured by branches. In the centre of the mill wall, at the top by the roof, there is a white weather-boarded projection called a lucam. Sacks of grain were hoisted off carts on a rope, up through a trapdoor in the bottom of the lucam and then stored.

In the foreground, the yellow farm track leads to the right, under the tree and round the edge of the mill-stream. At its lowest point this track was at times covered in tidal water, providing a splash for passing carts. The compact and level rust-coloured gravel bed, which guided cattle and wagons across the ford to Mill Meadow, shows through shallow mill-stream water.

White water churns forcefully out of the right culvert from under the mill, sending a strong current of white-tipped ripples across the mill-stream. Another culvert to the left in the shadows is still. Within each of these tunnels, out of sight in the mill building (page 11), is a wooden water-wheel 4 yards across (3.66m). The right wheel is turning, providing water power for grinding corn as the miller, standing in the doorway, takes a break.

10 Flatford Mill: a working corn mill
c.1890 photograph Suffolk Record Office
This photograph shows the white-washed working water-mill. The two wooden internal water wheels (page 11) had been replaced with a massive iron water-wheel which stood behind the mill (page 28).

11 Flatford Mill: a country residence
1936 photograph Suffolk Record Office
Stripped of milling machinery and iron water-wheel, plants adorn the walls. Another round-arched window has been built to the left of the central gable. Windows have also been introduced to the roof and to the white weather-boarded lucam, to bring more light into the residence.

Flatford Mill

Many of the earth embankments channelling water to Flatford Mill were constructed by the Saxons and, undoubtedly, a mill stood here before the Norman invasion. The Doomsday Book mentions a mill at 'Bercolt'. This early mill would have been a small timber building grinding corn after the harvest in the autumn and into the winter, using power from the river Stour swollen by winter rain. Roger Bigot, Earl of Norfolk, owned Flatford Mill between 1189 - 1221. It was managed at this time by the canons of Dodnash Priory who rented it to Nicholas of the Aldergrove.

For more than a century in the Georgian period, three generations of the Constable family owned Flatford Mill. These men were John Constable's great uncle Abram, his father Golding and younger brother Abram. John Constable had a deep and abiding affection for Flatford, born no doubt from the family involvement with the hamlet. Many of his paintings and drawings depict scenes at Flatford on the River Stour.

The first Constable to own Flatford Mill was a wealthy London corn merchant, Abram Constable. He bought Flatford Mill in 1742. A date-brick above and left of the mill door reads AC 1753. This was the year Abram Constable rebuilt the mill and extended the Millhouse. There is a date-stone on the back central gable of the mill which reads CAI 1733. The lettering has been tampered with and, had it not, would have read CAI 1753. C = Constable, A = Abram, I = Isabella (Abram's wife).

Abram Constable died in 1764, leaving the mill to his nephew, Golding Constable, who was twenty-six years old. Golding Constable was John Constable's father and, naturally enough, he wanted John to follow in his footsteps and become a corn merchant, as he and his uncle had before him. John tried the work for a year but it was simply not what he wanted to do. He was intent on being a painter and left for London to attend the Royal Academy school. His young brother Abram inherited the mill when their father died in 1816 and lived in the Millhouse with his wife Catherine and sister Mary.

The illustration (fig. 12) gives an artist's impression of how the mill may have looked during John Constable's lifetime. Flatford Mill was powered using two 12ft diameter x 3ft wide (3.66m x 0.92m) wooden water-wheels housed inside the mill. Each of the water-wheels was set in a channel (culvert). When sluices were raised at the back of the mill, water was released and flowed along the culverts. This pushed against the blades (floats) of the water-wheels and the wheels turned. The movement was conveying through a sturdy axle to simple wooden gearing and, finally, to pairs of millstones which were held on strong timber frames (Hursts) on the ground floor.

The steps in front of the mill door are built from two worn millstones, of chalcedonic hornstone quarried near Paris. Pieces of this stone were interlocked and cemented together with plaster of Paris, to form 4ft diameter x 1ft (1.22m x 0.3m) thick millstones. These were then bound with iron hoops and transported by Stour lighters (barges) up the river to the mill. They were regarded as the best type of millstones for grinding corn.

12 Flatford Mill cut-away showing the two timber water-wheels and gearing of Constable's time Robert Cook

13 Flatford Mill today

Valley Farm

John Constable 1827 Pencil drawing and wash 22.1 x 32.6cm (8¾ x 12⅞in) Private Collection

There are no known paintings, and only one drawing (above), by Constable of this very attractive building. It is tempting to speculate that there may have been a personality clash between the owner, John Lott, and John Constable. John Lott died on 13 January 1827 and, in October of that year, Constable took a holiday at Flatford with his eldest children, John and Minna, on their first trip to Suffolk. They stayed with John's brother and sister, Abram and Mary, in the Millhouse. In the picture (above) a woman and child stand next to the fence to the right and a cow is in front of the house. There is a doorway just to the right of the cross-wing that was the principal accommodation (the solar). The barn on the left is one of a collection of farmyard outbuildings which have been demolished, and all that remains of them now are scorch marks seen on the front lawn during dry summers.

14 Valley Farm before restoration 1924
Flatford Mill Photograph Collection
During restoration the modern porch and the ground floor bay window on the cross-wing were removed. So, too, the right chimney stack. The added doorway just to the right of the cross-wing was closed with vertical timbers.

Valley Farm

The illustration to the right (fig. 15) is of inside the medieval hall of Valley Farmhouse. The hall is the middle portion of the house. It is open to the rafters, smoke-blackened from open fires. This occurred before the inglenook fireplace with a massive white-washed, stepped, red brick chimney stack was built. The stack has been 'ghosted' in the illustration to show the central doors to the kitchen and food store (the service rooms) and, to the left, stairs to upper accommodation (the extra solar). The top of the stack is the chimney, seen most clearly in the drawing of Valley Farm by John Constable (page 12).

This timber-framed farmhouse has stood opposite Flatford Mill for more than 600 years. It was built to house a yeoman (a farmer) and his family who farmed adjoining fields and others over the river. The William Brasier map (fig. 16) shows the farmhouse and fields of Valley Farm in 1733 when it was owned by Edward Clark and known as Flatford Mill Farm. English Lott and his wife, Mary, grandparents of Willy Lott, had settled in the farmhouse as tenant farmers twenty-one years earlier in 1712, and raised their five children.

Why one of the fields on the map is called Church Field is shrouded in mystery. The most sensible explanation is that at one time it was owned by the parish church. Documents called glebe terriers, listing church land and other property going back to 1686, reveal nothing. A 'font' had been ploughed up in the field and examined by the county archaeologist, but it turned out to be a post-medieval mortar. So-called 'tombstones', similarly uncovered, were probably large slabs of naturally occurring stone known to be in the subsoil, called septaria or turtle stones. The *Church Field Mystery* remains unsolved.

15 Open Hall of Valley Farm with 'ghost' chimney stack Robert Cook

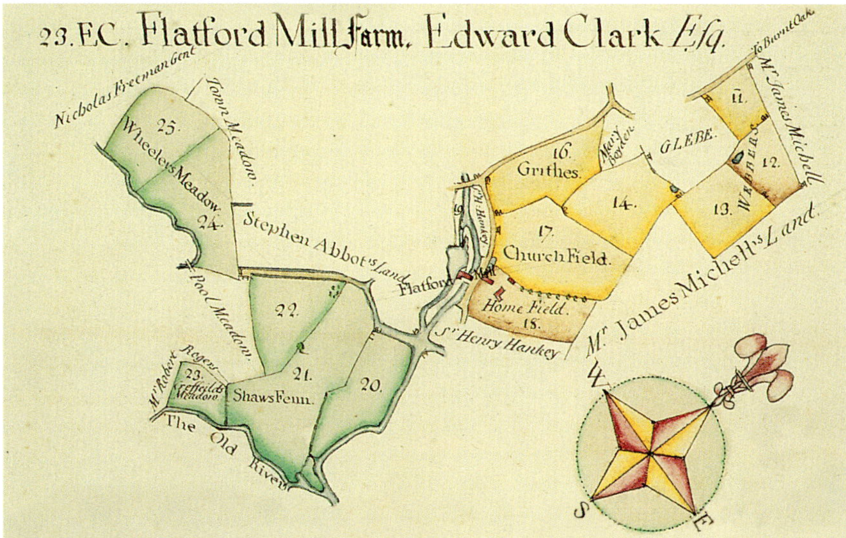

16 Flatford Mill Farm (Valley Farm) William Brasier 1733 Suffolk Record Office

17 Valley Farm today

Boat-building near Flatford Mill

John Constable 1814 Oil Painting 50.8 x 61.6cm (20 x 24 ¼in) V&A Picture Library London

John Constable made a few pencil sketches at the barge-building dry-dock in a small sketchbook during the late summer of 1814, including *Barge-building in the dock* (fig. 18) and *Men building a barge* (fig. 19). Soon after this, he went back to the dry-dock, set up his easel and painted most of *Boat-building near Flatford Mill* (above). His biographer, C R Leslie, wrote that Constable had said to him he had painted it *"entirely in the open air"*. Constable worked on this painting only in the afternoons and R B Beckett records, in Volume 1 of John Constable's correspondence, that the engraver David Lucas saying of Constable: *"he was always informed of the time to leave off by the film of smoke ascending from a chimney in the distance that the fire was lighted for the preparation of supper on the labourers return for the night"*.

In the sketch *Barge-building in the dock* (fig. 18) several men are working on the barge to make it watertight. Old hemp rope impregnated with tar (oakum) has been rolled by hand, pressed into the seams between the hull planking and driven home with caulking iron and mallet. The work done, a mallet rests against one of three timber stocks supporting the barge. A fire under the black cauldron has melted the pitch inside the cauldron. Dipping a mop into the molten pitch, a man would quickly carry the 'hot stuff' to the barge and work the mop head along the planking seam (paying up). A man on-board is perhaps measuring up, prior to making a cover-board for the bow. Other men are in the background.

In the finished oil painting *Boat-building near Flatford Mill* (above), Constable chose to include, from the small collection of figures in the sketch, *Men building a barge* (fig. 19), a figure of a seated boy rolling oakum, and the two cauldrons with a pitch mop. This is at odds with the condition of the barge shown in the finished oil painting. In this the seams are all caulked and paid up, and the caulking mallet and other tools now lie outside the dock. There is no need for more oakum or pitch and the figure of the boy rolling oakum has a superimposed quality. Constable may have referred to his sketch *Men building a barge* and added the figure for artistic effect in his studio. It is, therefore, unlikely he painted *Boat-building near Flatford Mill* entirely outdoors.

Other incidents in the finished work are the man on the far left bundling long punting poles (quants) while, nearby, another works on a curved cover-board. A barge glides silently by, towed by the chestnut horse on the far river-bank as a little girl leaves down a path to Bridge Cottage.

18 *Barge-building in the dock* John Constable
7 September 1814 Pencil Sketch
8 x 10.8cm (3⅛ x 4¼in)
V&A Picture Library London

19 *Men building a barge* John Constable 1814
Pencil Sketch 8 x 10.8cm (3⅛ x 4¼in)
V&A Picture Library London

View on the Stour near Dedham

John Constable 1821 First Version 'Oil Sketch' 129.4 x 185.3cm (51 x 73in) Private Collection

Constable called this six foot painting 'the Bridge'. In September 1821, he was working on it at his Hampstead Village home and wrote to his friend John Fisher *"I am so much behind hand with the Bridge, which I have great hindrances in. I cannot do it here- & I must leave my family & work in London"*. The following month he wrote to Fisher *"I am most anxious to get into my London painting room, for I do not consider myself at work without I am before a six foot canvas"*. Constable may have referred to the sketch (fig. 20) from his 1814 sketchbook. When Fisher came by and saw the painting, during January 1822, the main Stour lighter had a sail. Constable later painted this out and traces of it can be seen above the lighterman hoisting the anchor. The raised mast and lowered sail on the moored lighter were painted for artistic effect. The mast would have in fact been lowered to pass under the galley beams that spanned Flatford Lock and remain lowered to pass under Flatford Bridge. Constable painted out a lighterman from the stern of the main lighter and also a cowherd and cow from the bridge. The cow was repainted, to the right. It would appear from all the changes he made in this painting that it was not progressing well.

20 *Flatford Old Bridge and Dedham Church from the barge-building dock* John Constable 1814
Pencil sketch 8 x 10.8cm (3⅛ x 4¼in) V&A Picture Library
The stern of a lighter (bottom right) is that of the one being built in *Boat-building near Flatford Mill* (opposite page 15).

View on the Stour near Dedham

John Constable 1822 Finished Version Oil Painting 130 x 188cm (51 x 74in) Huntington Library, Art Collections and Botanical Gardens San Marino California

This certainly seems to have been the case because, soon after Fisher's visit, Constable abandoned the picture and pressed on with another canvas of the scene which became the finished version of the oil painting (above).

At the beginning of April 1822 a letter to Fisher read *"The composition is almost totally changed from what you saw. I have taken away the sail, added another barge in the middle of the picture, with a principal figure, altered the group of trees, and made the bridge entire. The picture now has a rich centre, and the right-hand side becomes only an accessory".*

And on the 13th April
"I have sent my large picture to the Academy. I never worked so hard before & now time was so short for me-it wanted much-but still I hope the work in it is better than any I have yet done".

21 *Two sketches on one page of men poling barges*
John Constable 1813 Pencil sketch
8.9 x 12cm (3½ x 4¾in) V&A Picture Library
Source of the principal figure.

22 Gang of lighters at Great Horkesley on the Stour c1900 John Marriage Photograph Collection

Stour Lighters

Lighters transported cargo along the River Stour navigation from 1713 for more than 200 years. The 23 mile horse-drawn journey downriver from Sudbury to Brantham, and the additional 2 miles of the estuary on the tide to Mistley, took about two days. Lighters carried down river bricks, wheat and barley, among other things, and, up river, the cargo was mainly coal, marl and London horse manure.

There were a few single lighters but most worked in pairs called 'gangs' (figures 22 & 23 and the book cover). Locks on the River Stour were able to accommodate a gang. The stern of the lead lighter was chained to the bow of the second. A huge steering pole, fixed to the bow of the second lighter, extended forward to the cockpit amidships of the lead lighter. From there, the skipper steered the gang using the rear lighter as a rudder. Rear lighters usually had a single hold and small cabin.

John Constable's oil painting *Barge-building near Flatford Mill* (opposite page 15) is an example of a lighter, owned by his father Golding Constable, being built in the dry dock at Flatford. The ingenious method of draining the dock, used also to keep it free of water while work was underway, either on repair or new construction, is shown in the illustration (fig. 24), as is the flooding of the dock to launch the vessel.

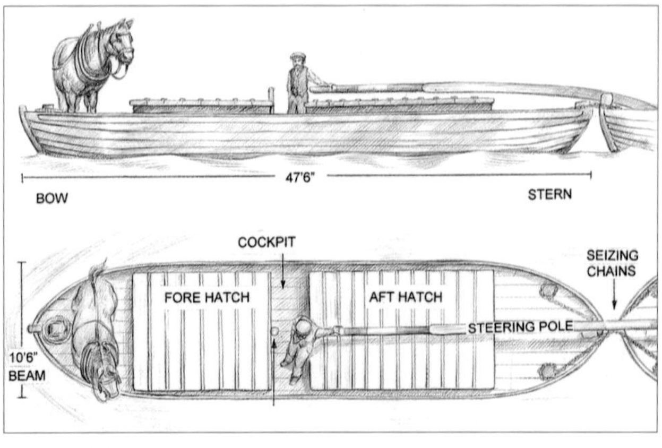

23 Stour lighter gang Robert Cook

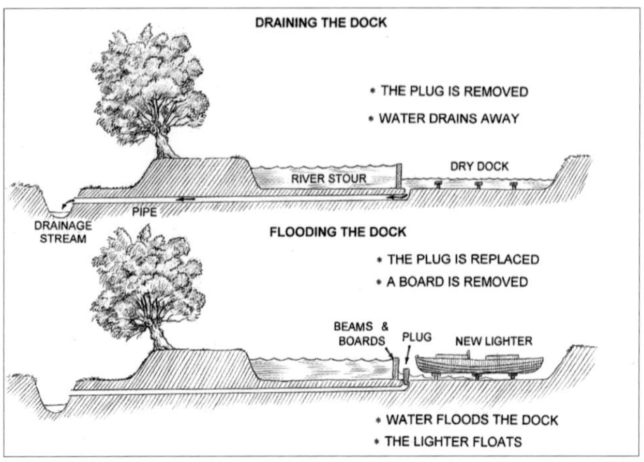

24 Flatford dry-dock Robert Cook

25 Bridge Cottage from Tunnel Lane c1900 photograph Suffolk Record Office

Bridge Cottage and Flatford Bridge

Bridge Cottage stands prominently at the entrance of Flatford hamlet on a corner at the bottom of Tunnel Lane. To the right is Flatford Bridge over the Stour. To the left, the lane to Flatford Mill, Valley Farm and Willy Lott's House. Bridge Cottage consists of a single storey with attic rooms and was home to two families, ten members of which are enjoying a photocall on their doorsteps (fig. 25). Each family had half the cottage, inside of which there would have been a wooden partition between the red brick stack and the two doors. When first built early in the seventeenth century, Bridge Cottage may have originally been a single small house with a hall open to the rafters. The kitchen and food store (the service) would have been located in the far left end of the house. Next to this would have been the sitting room (the parlour), then the brick chimney (the stack bay) and the right half, the Open Hall. The main entrance would have been a doorway between the present two doors (which were then absent) situated opposite the stack, giving a 'baffle-entry'. Round the back of the cottage, midway, there are two brick arches in the brick wall, the last remains of the bread oven extension.

At first glance, the old photograph (fig. 26) gives the impression of a scene remarkably unchanged since John Constable painted here early in the nineteenth century. However, there are a number of significant changes. The gang of barges is being towed down a widened river towards the new lock (off photo - page 23) built parallel to the one seen in Constable's paintings. Two people are standing on a wooden bridge that has two sets of support piles, rather than the one set seen in Constable's paintings. Bridge Cottage has gained an out-building and a backcloth of elms.

26 Lighters at Flatford c1905 photograph Essex Record Office

Flatford Mill: Scene on a navigable river

John Constable 1817 Oil Painting 101.7 x 127cm (40 x 50in) Tate Gallery London

This painting captures a moment in a working day on the river. The scene is the Stour at Flatford from a high vantage point on the embanked side of Flatford Bridge, looking down the towpath, to Flatford Lock and Flatford Mill. The horse in the foreground, with a barge boy astride, has just walked along the towpath pulling a gang of lighters out of the lock and up the river to the bridge. The boy and a man on the rear lighter look on as the horse is untied. Under the momentum of the pull, the gang have drifted into a gentle jack-knife and are being poled straight, to pass under Flatford Bridge.

The composition of the final oil painting originated as a pencil tracing (fig. 27). Constable looked through a sheet of glass he had placed on his easel in front of the Flatford scene. He painted an outline of the view, in ink, on the glass and laid squared paper over the wet ink. The outline soaked into the back of the paper and through to the front where he traced it in pencil.

Constable also drew inspiration for the final oil painting from an oil sketch (fig. 28) of the view. He copied his pencil tracing onto a squared canvas and then painted the oil sketch while in front of the scene. It shows all the main features of the tracing, except the lighters have been removed and two horses added. Constable would have referred to both the pencil tracing and oil sketch in order to compose the finished picture.

This painting contains many closely observed figures engaged in all manner of activity and other beautifully observed details: the barge boy's hat and whip on the ground between the two mooring posts; the clear water of the drainage stream and its fringe of flowers; magpies and the reaper in Bridge Meadow; cows beyond the reaper in Mill Meadow; two young anglers on the towpath; other boys fishing in the lock; Abram Constable's garden fence on the island to the left of the lock; a barge moored by the mill; the warning bell on the ridge above; and on the far left, Valley Farm's white-washed cross-wing.

27 *Flatford Mill* John Constable 1816
Pencil Tracing 25.5 x 31.2cm (19 x 12¼in)
Tate Gallery London

28 *Flatford Mill* John Constable 1816
Oil Sketch 34.3 x 41.3cm (13½ x 16¼in)
David Thomson

29 *Granary Barn at Flatford* John Constable
10 July 1813 Pencil Sketch 8.9 x 12cm (3½ x 4¾in)
V&A Picture Library London

30 Flatford Steam Mill Robert Cook

Flatford Steam Mill

John Constable drew the sketch of his father's Granary Barn (fig. 29) in 1814, at a time well before the dominance of steam-power. Barges full of grain were moored in the wet dock close by and unloaded and stored in the barn destined to be ground into flour at Flatford Water Mill. The granary is reflected on the water and, on the right, a couple of trees are growing on the end of the island.

Many years later, corn stored in the barn was no longer carted the short distance to Flatford Water Mill. A steam-powered mill was built onto the barn, possibly by William Rufus Bentall (page 29), and the grain was ground by Flatford Steam Mill.

At some time between 1846 and 1879, a brick extension was built along the back of the thatched Granary Barn to house a steam-engine, boiler and other steam-mill machinery. The coal-fired steam-mill powered pairs of millstones held in place on timber 'Hurst Frames' (page 29). Coal for the boiler was carried up the Stour in lighters that were steered using long poles (quants) into the wet-dock. The coal was unloaded onto the mill wharf and stored in the shed next door to the steam-mill.

The illustration (fig. 30) gives an artist's impression of how the steam-mill may have looked when viewed from across the Stour. The photograph (fig. 31) shows the steam-mill had a pitched roof and a round-arched window with radial glazing in the gable-end. It also shows the position and construction of the chimney stack base. The chimney stack can be seen in the distance in the photograph (fig. 32).

Walter Benneworth owned Flatford water-mill and steam-mill in 1879. In 1896, Arthur John Benneworth owned the steam-mill and William Green the water-mill. Competition for work was short-lived. The water-mill ceased working in 1901, whereas the steam-mill continued working until about 1929.

31 Flatford Steam Mill ruin
July 1965 photograph
Suffolk Record Office

32 Flatford Steam Mill chimney
c1900 photograph
Derek Tripp Photograph Collection

33 Granary Barn is now a museum

34 DETAIL *Flatford Mill* John Constable 1817 Tate Gallery London

35 DETAIL Gang of lighters at Flatford Lock c1905 photograph Essex Record Office

36 The old and new position of Flatford Lock Robert Cook

Flatford Lock

Between 1705 and 1713, work was undertaken to make the river Stour navigable. All watermills on the lower 23 miles of the river were bypassed from Sudbury to the Brantham tide-mill. Thirteen locks (two sets of double gates separated by a chamber) were built and thirteen staunches (one set of double doors) raised the water level, so that Stour lighters, each with a load of 13 tons, were able to navigate the Stour. One of these original locks was Flatford Old Lock.

Flatford Old Lock had a sloping turf chamber which required a lot of water to fill, and indeed it soaked up a substantial amount. At each end of the lock a pair of gates hung on posts which extended above the lock chamber. The tops of these jointed into a horizontal galley beam (also called a lock lintel) and the bottom of the lock posts jointed under water into a timber sill. This four-sided frame prevented the very heavy timber gates dislodging the lock posts. There may have been supporting frames on either side of the main lock gate frames. In 1776, the year Constable was born, the turf lock at Flatford was replaced by an elaborate timber-framed chamber. This is the lock seen in John Constable's paintings. There were no less than nine galley beams spaced along the chamber All nine can be seen in John Dunthorne's painting (fig. 37).

Flatford New Lock was built in 1838, the year after Constable died, and the old lock chamber was filled in to became part of the island. Both lock positions are shown on the aerial illustration (fig. 36). Compare the relative positions of the two locks in the detail from Constable's *Flatford Mill* (fig. 34) and the detail from the old photograph (fig. 35). The new lock had a simpler timber-framed construction which has since been replaced by the present concrete chamber, and four decorative galley beams. The first step towards building the new lock occurred when the proprietors of the Stour Navigation commissioned Mr Cubitt to undertake a survey of the condition of the Navigation. His report, dated 22 June 1836, states "*Flatford Lock The floors of this lock lie 2 feet too high, it should be rebuilt on the South side parallel to the present one, which would remove it further from the Waste Gates of the Mill and give a much better entrance to the lock*". The proprietors agreed with him and contracted the work on a new lock for £700. Mr Cubitt reported again in 1839 "*Flatford Lock This lock is quite new and very good but the Shoals just below this Lock are very bad, and at this time cause an entire stoppage of the trade*". This was a reference to the ford.

37 DETAIL *Flatford Lock* John Dunthorne 1814 Oil Painting Colchester Museum Viewed from the millpool end.

The Lock

John Constable 1824 Oil Painting 142.2 x 120.7cm (56 x 47½in) Carmen Thyssen-Bornemisza Madrid

A man in a bright red waistcoat and rolled shirt-sleeves commands attention in the middle of the painting. He strikes a dynamic stance, energetically turning the hoisting bar with a wooden handspike. His physical activity is the impressive and powerful focus of the painting. The chain below winds round the bar, lifting a wooden paddle that lets water out of the lock. The man has almost lifted the right paddle. Water in the lock chamber is escaping and, as it does so, it churns the millpool below.

Aboard the lighter in the lock chamber, the skipper has a steadying rope wound round a bollard and is being watched by a woman from the galley amidships. The boy rider, beside the chestnut tow-horse and a spaniel, waits for the water level to drop and is ready to heave on a chain to open the left lock gate, as the man opposite him pulls open the right gate. The barge will then have free passage out of Flatford Lock .

Incomplete multiple posts and galley beams are seen in the preliminary pencil sketch (fig. 38). Constable included them in the full-scale sketch in oils that then followed (not shown), but subsequently changed his mind and painted out the lock superstructure. The repetitious vertical posts and horizontal galley beams would have dominated the picture and were therefore pictorially unacceptable. Without them, we are able to look past Flatford Lock across the vale to Dedham Church tower in the distance. Flatford Lock is seen from a low, close viewpoint across the millpool, from John Constable's younger brother Abram's garden behind Flatford Millhouse.

Constable sold this painting on the opening day of the 1824 Royal Academy Summer Show. He wrote to his friend John Fisher on the 8th May 1824 *"My picture is liked at the Academy. Indeed it forms a decided feature and its light cannot be put out, because it is the light of nature - the Mother of all that is valuable in poetry, painting or anything else - where an appeal to the soul is required. The language of the heart is the only one that is universal.... My execution annoys most of them and all the scholastic ones - perhaps the sacrifices I make for lightness and brightness is too much, but these things are the essence of landscape".*

38 *Flatford Lock* John Constable 1823
Pencil and wash 16.8 x 30cm (6⅝ x 11¾in)
David Thomson
A preliminary drawing for *The Lock*. The hunched figure is using a handspike in the lock paddle hoisting bar on the far side of the lock. Three galley beams span the lock. Another at the far left end of the lock is missing. Constable drew one of its upright posts.

Flatford Mill from the lock

John Constable 1812 Oil painting 63.5 x 90.2cm (25 x 35 ½in) David Thomson

The view (above) is from the towpath beside Old Flatford Lock (Flatford Map & page 23), looking downriver to the Lombardy poplars reflected in the water in the middle distance. About half Flatford Mill and all of the Millhouse are depicted on the left bank. On the right bank, cows graze in the corner of Bridge Field in the shade of trees. Two boys are fishing in the millpool. One boy in a yellow waistcoat stands holding onto a lock post. His friend in a red jacket sits on the towpath leaning on the timber barge barrier, waiting for a bite. Only the lower lock gates posts and galley beam are shown. The lock chamber is empty and the chains on the gates will be pulled to open the gates to admit the Stour lighter moored to the left bank of the River Stour. Two figures are aboard the lighter and another in a white shirt is just ashore.

Constable exhibited this painting at the Royal Academy in 1812, calling it 'A Water-mill'. He wrote to Maria Bicknell on 24 April 1812 telling her that Benjamin West, Royal Academy President, had liked his painting *"I wished to know if he considered that mode of study as laying the foundations of real excellence. "Sir" (said he) "I consider that you have attained it".*

During the two years prior to the exhibition, Constable visited and revisited the site to paint a series of at least six oil sketches. He tried compositions showing different parts of the panorama. At the left end of the range he showed Flatford Mill, the Millhouse and the river - but no meadows. While at the right end of the range, one of the sketches shows the meadows and river, but no Millhouse or mill. (these two pictures are not shown).

Only one of the six sketches (fig. 40) is painted from the left side of the lock. Another point of interest about this sketch is that in the centre of the mill wall near the roof there is a white weather-boarded lucam. Lighters would have moored under it and their sacks of wheat would have been hoisted up into it. This lucam matches one on the other side of the mill seen in *Flatford Mill from Willy Lott's House* (opposite page 9). The finished painting (above) is based mainly on another sketch (fig. 39). The figure in the red waistcoat had been painted by Constable, in other oil sketches, with a brown shirt and then a blue shirt, and, finally painted out of the finished painting with traces of red paint remaining.

39 *Flatford Mill from the lock* John Constable
1812 Oil Sketch 24.8 x 29.8cm (9¾ x 11¾in)
V&A Picture Library London

40 *Flatford Mill from the lock* John Constable
1812 Oil Sketch 15.2 x 21.2cm (6 x 8⅜in)
David Thomson

41 Flatford Mill showing the wheelhouse Pre-1907 photograph Suffolk Record Office

42 Wheelhouse cut-away with massive iron water-wheel Robert Cook

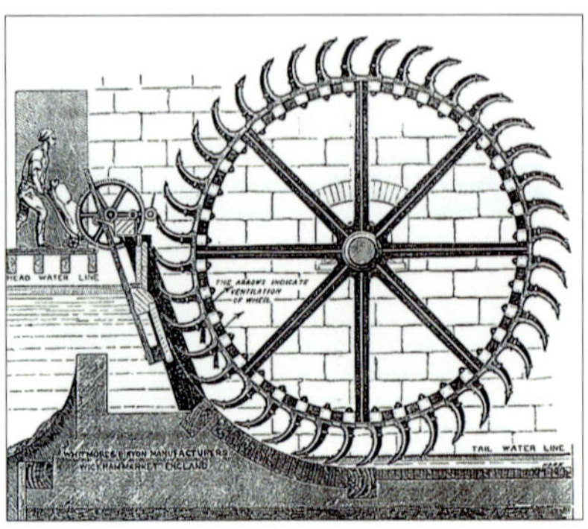

43 Side view of an iron water-wheel
Whitmore & Binyon 1879 catalogue
The water-wheel at Flatford would have been a similar size. It dwarfs the miller wheeling a sack of corn.

44 Flatford Mill Today
In about 1907 the wheelhouse, water-wheel and offal room were removed.

Flatford Mill

John Constable died in 1837 and, therefore, would never have seen the massive undershot water-wheel (fig. 42) on the north side of the mill. It was installed by Whitmore and Binyon for the miller William Rufus Bentall (fig. 47) some time between 1849-1862.

This great wheel was probably the largest on the River Stour and must have been a tremendous sight when turning. It was made of iron and measured 16ft diameter by almost 14ft wide (4.57m x 4.27m) with 40 curved metal open-ended buckets. The long single-storey wheelhouse attached to the mill had a kitchen work room (scullery) at the end nearest the millpool, the water-wheel was in the middle and a room containing corn chaff (offal room) was beyond the wheel.

Until the mill ceased working in 1901, the brick room on the far left in the photograph (fig. 41) contained flour ready to be loaded into barges that moored alongside. This room is attached to a weather-boarded flour room (and granary), with a double-sloped (mansard) roof.

On the ridge between the two rooms is a warning bell which rang automatically when the water level behind the mill became dangerously high. High water ran down a wood trough (leat) and turned a little waterwheel. A crank on the wheel axle was attached to a cable from the bell. When the bell sounded, the miller was warned to raise the floodgates that are under the boardwalk, left of the wheelhouse. White water is coming from them in the photograph (fig. 41). High water was also a good time for the miller to open the sluice to the huge water-wheel and to get to work grinding corn.

45 *Interior of Flatford Mill* Thomas Pyne 1891 Water-colour Ipswich Museums and Galleries

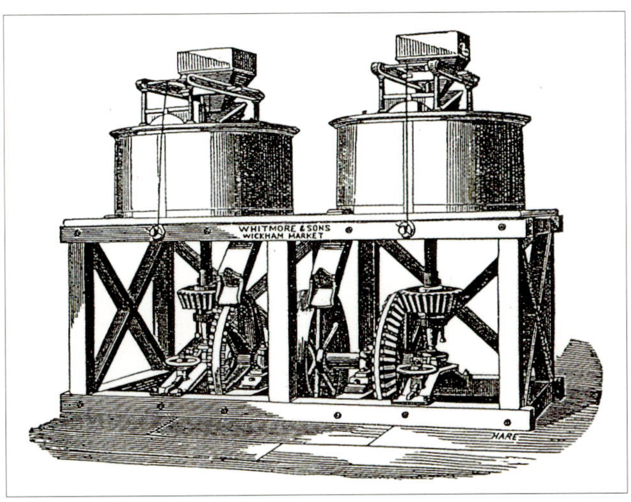

46 Double wood-framed Hurst Whitmore & Binyon 1879 catalogue

When the exterior iron water-wheel was installed, the two internal timber water-wheels and gearing used by the Constable family (page 11) were removed from Flatford Mill. The new water-wheel was so huge it undoubtedly would have driven at least four pairs of millstones. The illustration (fig. 46) shows a Whitmore & Binyon double wood-framed Hurst. Two of these double Hursts would have been installed. Each of these carried two pairs of stones. The heavy timber framework supported the millstones at shoulder level and enclosed the main gearing. The watercolour painting by Thomas Pyne (fig. 45) is of the inside of Flatford Mill in 1891. The right half of one enclosed double wood-framed Hurst can be seen. Stones and gearing are boarded-in and a number 2 is painted on the millstone casing. The second double Hurst is opposite the miller out of sight behind the brick partition wall.

William Bentall married Ann Lott (1824-1904) who was raised at Flatford in Valley Farm and whose great uncle was Willy Lott. William Bentall and Stephen Durrant Lott (Ann's brother) bought Flatford Mill from John Constable's young brother Abram in 1846. Stephen Lott sold his share of the property to William Bentall the following year and emigrated to Australia. Bentall decided to modernise the mill machinery. (and probably installed the Steam Mill – page 22) Later millers operating both the water and steam mills were Richard Barrell (c1865-1875) and Walter Benneworth (c1879-1892). Competition for work began in 1896 when William Green worked the water-mill, while Arthur John Benneworth ran the steam-mill. Lancelot Docura was the owner of the water-mill when it ceased working in 1901. It was converted into a country residence (fig.11) and, after the Second World War, it was given to the National Trust and leased to the Field Studies Council.

47 William Rufus Bentall (1823-1905)
J Brian Lott Lott Family Archive

The White Horse

John Constable 1819 Oil Painting 131.5 x 187.8cm (51¾ x 74in) Frick Collection New York

Activity in this large painting is well to the left where the white horse aboard a Stour lighter is being 'boated' from one side of the River Stour to the other. In the 1819 Royal Academy Exhibition, Constable gave the painting the nondescript title *A Scene on the river Stour.* Constable's biographer C R Leslie quotes from a letter by Constable, written in the 1830's which contained no mention of horse or barge *"one of my happiest efforts on a large scale, being a placid representation of a serene grey morning, summer"*. Constable at times referred to the painting as 'The Farm Yard'. It was left to Constable's good friend John Fisher to give the painting this nickname by which it has became known. It was a success at the Royal Academy Show and regarded by Constable as one of his most important paintings, not least because it led to his election as an Associate of the Royal Academy.

Immediately prior to the scene observed in the painting, the white horse had towed the single lighter downriver a short distance from Flatford Lock. The lighter was moored on the right bank, just left of the timber fence and barge barrier seen bottom left in the picture. The horse stepped aboard into the bow well and the barge was poled mid-stream by two lightermen. The skipper is at the helm, relaxed and smoking a pipe, while the tow-horse boy is hauling the rope aboard. They are on the tidal reach of the river at high tide and are straightening up, ready to set course downriver assisted by the river current and possibly on an ebb tide. The boated horse is taking a well-earned rest. Downriver (off picture) it will step ashore onto the towpath on the left bank and resume towing the lighter to Brantham Lock.

In the picture, on the opposite bank, is the white-washed rear gable of Gibeon's farmhouse. This house was occupied by tenant farmer William Lott, and naturally enough it would have been known locally as 'Willy Lott's House'. The house, minus the lean-to, can be seen in the photograph (fig. 49). The rowing boat next to the thatched boat shelter is moored at the exit of the mill-stream. Constable referred to the sketch (fig. 2) of a rowing boat for this painting and three years later used it again in *The Haywain* (opposite page 5). Behind the tree, to the right of the boat shelter, is the large thatched barn had an attached smaller barn which housed a trap and a plough stands in the yard.

The White Horse was a new departure for John Constable in scale, location and technique. It was the largest picture he had completed to date and the first of six large River Stour scenes he called his 'six-foot' pictures (five of them were about 6 x 4ft). What was also new was that it was painted entirely in his 'painting room' in London and, for the first time, Constable undertook a preliminary full-scale oil sketch.

48 White Horse on a Stour lighter c1900
Bob Horlock Photograph Collection
Boating tow-horses across the river on Stour lighters continued into the early twentieth century.

49 Rear of Willy Lott's House today

Walking in Constable Country

Walking through, 'Constable Country', could not be easier. Arriving at Manningtree Railway Station, the view from the platform is across Cattawade Marshes nature reserve. Flatford is only two miles (3km) away. Follow the path marked on the Constable Country map (opposite page). The walk takes you along tracks to the River Stour and atop the river embankment, which guides you to Flatford hamlet while giving you an elevated view over the nature reserve. Only a mile further along easy paths brings you to East Bergholt village where John Constable was born, or to Dedham village where he went to school.

Manningtree railway station is the 'Gateway to Constable Country'. It is a mainline station less than an hour from London Liverpool Street and from Norwich. It is also accessible from Cambridge via Ipswich and from the Continent via Harwich. As well as easy access to Flatford, East Bergholt and Dedham, the station is a starting place for adventurous long walks through Essex and Suffolk. These paths are the Essex Way, Painters Way, St.Edmund Way, Stour Valley Path, Suffolk Coast and Heaths Path and Suffolk Way.

Flatford has a permanent Constable exhibition in Bridge Cottage and a National Trust shop and cafe next door, with a bicycle park near the dry-dock. There is a Visitor Information Centre with a public toilet and parking spaces for disabled drivers. A pay to park car park is provided nearby. Along the lane is the Granary Museum and at Flatford Mill the Field Studies Council run environment and art and craft courses. The River Stour Trust offer river trips in an electric-powered boat. Or you may prefer to hire a rowing boat, or arrive by canoe.

Further Reading

R B Beckett (ed) *John Constable's Correspondence* Suffolk Records Society 1962-1968
Volume 1 *The Family at East Bergholt 1801-1837*
Volume 2 *Early Friends and Maria Bicknell (Mrs Constable)*
Volume 3 *The Correspondence with C R Leslie RA*
Volume 4 *Patrons, Dealers and Fellow Artists*
Volume 5 *Various Friends, with Charles Boner and the Artist's children*
Volume 6 *The Fishers*
R B Beckett (ed) *John Constable's Discourses* Suffolk Records Society 1970
John French *Suffolk Flatford Yesterdays* Stylus Press
Edward Jackson and Wendy Morgan *Flatford: A Contrasting UK Locality* Geographical Association. 1996
Charles R Leslie *Memoirs of the life of John Constable RA* 1843; Jonathan Mayne (ed) Phaidon 1951
Leslie Parris, Conal Shields and Ian Fleming-Williams *John Constable: Further Documents and Correspondence* Suffolk Records Society 1975
Leslie Parris, Ian Fleming-Williams and Conal Shields *Constable: Paintings, Watercolours & Drawings* Tate 1976
Leslie Parris and Ian Fleming-Williams *Constable* Tate Gallery 1991
Graham Reynolds *The Early Paintings and Drawings of John Constable* Yale University Press 1996
Graham Reynolds *The Later Paintings and drawings of John Constable* Yale University Press 1984
River Stour Trust *The Essex and Suffolk River Stour* 1989
N G Rogers *The Valley of the Stour from Weston Green to Harwich* Ian Henry 1992
Michael Rosenthal *Constable: The Painter and his Landscape* Yale University Press 1983
Alastair Smart and Attfield Brooks *Constable and his Country* Elak 1976
Henry de Salis *Bradshaw's Canals and Rivers of England and Wales* Blacklock 1904 (David & Charles 1969)
Ambrose J Waller *The Suffolk Stour* Adlard 1957
East Bergholt Society Archive Courtesy of Patricia Wright
Lott Family Archive Courtesy of J Brian Lott
River Stour Trust Archive Courtesy of Anthony Platt
Simmons Collection Courtesy of Peter Dolman
'Flatford Lock...2ft too high' Suffolk Record Office. Bury St.Edmunds EE501/13/32
'Flatford Lock...is quite new' Suffolk Record Office. Bury St.Edmunds EE501/13/32